A LITTLE

SPICE
COOKBOOK

MARILYN BRIGHT

Illustrated by LYNDA STEWART

CHRONICLE BOOKS
SAN FRANCISCO

First published in 1995 by
The Appletree Press Ltd
19–21 Alfred Street
Belfast BT2 8DL
Tel. +44 (0) 1232 243074
Fax +44 (0) 1232 246756

A Little Spice Cookbook

Jacket design by Karen Smidth.

First published in the United States in 1996
by
Chronicle Books,
275 Fifth Street, San Francisco,
California 94103

ISBN 0-8118-1292-8

9 8 7 6 5 4 3 2 1

Introduction

Spices – the very word conjures up rich images of gold and silks and perfumes of the Orient. For centuries, the spice trade created fortunes and built wealthy cities like Venice where the busy harbor funneled precious cargoes to the West.

Until new routes and better transport opened up Eastern trade, spices were the prerogative of the wealthy, precious substances to be kept under lock and key. It seems incredible to us now that the peppercorns in every corner shop might once have been the price of a doge's palace, or that the cinnamon we scatter on an apple tart could have been a princess's dowry.

The spices that seem quite usual to us now would have astounded even our own grandmothers. Travel and modern living have introduced us to cuisines as far flung as Punjabi and Portuguese, Jamaican and Japanese. In all cases, the wonderful differences are made up from a rich palette of spices and seasonings, a palette that is available to us all to explore and enjoy.

A note on measures

The strength of spices varies according to source and growing conditions as well as age and storage, so measurements given in recipes should be adjusted according to taste. Recipes are for four servings unless otherwise indicated.

The Spice Cupboard

Allspice These small dried berries are sometimes called Jamaica pepper. They seem to combine flavors of cinnamon, cloves, and nutmeg, and are useful in sweet and savory mixtures, for pickling and for sausages.

Anise or Aniseed Light brown, elongated seeds, familiar flavoring for hard sweets and liqueurs such as sambuca and French pastis. Excellent seasoning for seafood and shellfish. There is also a very pretty star anise used in Chinese cooking.

Cardamom These small, aromatic seeds are encased in papery green pods or bleached white pods that are removed before the spice is ground for use. Primarily used in Indian dishes, occasionally in Russian and Scandinavian baked sweets.

Cinnamon The fragrant bark of a tropical tree, cinnamon is usually sold in rolled sticks or quills. Used mainly for baking and sweets in the West, it is widely used in Eastern cooking in stews and chicken and lamb dishes.

Coriander These round, light brown seeds have a sweetish aroma, considered essential in curry powders, and are often used as seasoning for pork dishes and sausage mixtures.

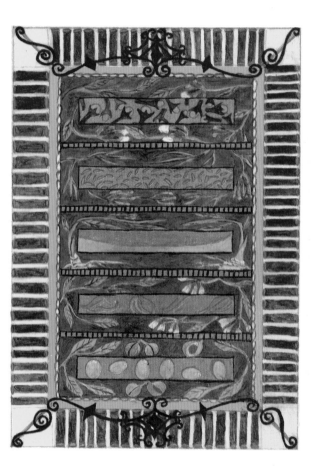

Cloves The brown, nail-shaped buds of a tropical tree, cloves are strongly fragrant and are used in spicy cakes, Christmas puddings, and mincemeat, where their preservative qualities were once a consideration. Use sparingly in bread sauce, baked hams, and long-cooked stews.

Cumin These warmly aromatic, light brown seeds are prized in Indian and Mexican cooking. Essential in *chili con carne, couscous,* and many curries.

Ginger This hand-shaped root is the underground rhizome of a tropical Asian plant, used fresh, preserved, dried, or ground. With fresh and peppery-spicy flavor, it is widely used in oriental cooking and in a range of sweet and savoury dishes, pickles, and confectionery.

Mace and Nutmeg Mace blades are the lacy husks enclosing the hard, round nutmeg, and both have a pleasingly sweet aroma, although the flavor of mace is more subtle. Nutmeg is best freshly grated and is used in cooked fruit and custard-based sweets as well as creamy sauces like béchamel. Mace can be ground in a mill and is used similarly in cakes, desserts, and soufflés.

Mustard These black and brown or yellow seeds are used finely ground in curry mixtures as well as in the popular, zesty condiment, which is produced in many strengths. Mustard powder is also used in sauces, and egg and cheese dishes, while the white seeds are used in pickling mixtures.

Pepper Reputedly the oldest and most important spice in the world, pepper is available as dried ripe black peppercorns, unripe green peppercorns with milder flavor, or white pepper from which the outer husk has been removed. Pink peppercorns are not true peppers but blend well with the others. Likewise, Szechuan pepper is another type of dried berry used in Chinese seasonings. Although generally used dried and ground or cracked, the green form of peppercorn is sometimes pickled and used for sauces and pâtés.

Saffron The most expensive spice, saffron is made up of the threadlike red stigmas of crocus flowers, producing a rich yellow coloring and mildly pungent aroma. A tiny pinch of saffron is sufficient for most dishes and should be crushed and soaked in liquid to be added to food. Especially useful for fish dishes, breads, and cakes, and essential for paella and bouillabaisse.

Turmeric A rhizome related to ginger, turmeric is generally sold dried and ground as a bright orange-gold powder. It is often substituted for the more expensive saffron for coloring, but has its own warm and mildly aromatic flavor. Turmeric is used in curry powder, pickling mixtures, rice dishes, and many Indian and Eastern specialities.

Vanilla The deliciously scented black vanilla beans are the seed pods of a Mexican orchid. Most commonly available in an alcohol-based extract, vanilla infused directly from the pod has a far superior flavor, and the black seeds ground with a little sugar have the most intense flavor of all. Whole pods infused in hot milk can be rinsed, dried, and stored in sugar for re-use. Vanilla is used widely in sweets and desserts, and has special affinity for chocolate.

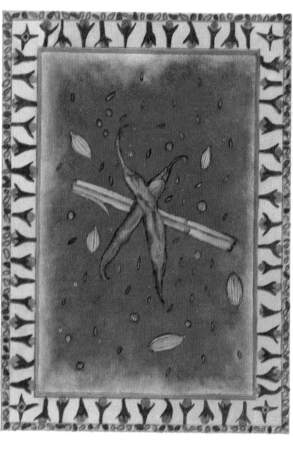

Classic Mixtures

Certain classic combinations of spices are so successful that they have become part of the international cooks' repertoire. Freshly ground and blended mixtures will be far superior to commercially prepared ones. Always allow for adjustment to individual taste.

Curry Powder

There are thousands of variations of this popular Indian seasoning. The following blend is spicy, but not too hot. If liked, heat can be added with extra chilis, fresh or dried.

---

3 tbsp coriander seeds	2-in cinnamon stick,
1 tbsp cumin seed	broken up
1 tbsp mustard seed	1/2 tsp grated nutmeg
1 tsp cardamom seeds	1–2 dried red chili peppers
(pods removed)	2 tbsp ground turmeric
8 whole cloves	

Preheat oven to 350°F. Combine coriander, cumin, mustard, cardamom, cloves, and cinnamon in a shallow baking tray, and place in oven. Toast spices for 8 to 10 minutes, shaking tray several times. Allow spices to cool, then combine with remaining ingredients and grind to fine powder in a spice mill or electric coffee grinder. Store in an airtight container if not used immediately.

Mixed Spice

The traditional English mixture for Christmas puddings, cakes, and biscuits; useful for stewed fruits and many other dishes.

3 tsp coriander seeds	12 whole cloves
2-in cinnamon stick, broken up	3 tsp freshly grated nutmeg
	2 tsp ground ginger

Grind coriander, cinnamon, and cloves in a spice mill or electric coffee grinder until very fine. Combine with remaining spices and store in an airtight container.

Pickling Spice

This mixture is usually steeped in warmed vinegar to use in pickles and relishes.

> 2 2-in cinnamon sticks, broken up
> 1 tbsp yellow mustard seeds
> 1 tbsp whole black peppercorns
> 1 tsp allspice berries
> 1 tsp whole cloves
> 1 tsp coriander seeds
> 1 tsp mace blades, broken up
> 4 bay leaves, broken up
> 1 small dried red chili, broken up

Combine spices, and store in airtight container.

Quatre Épices

The French "four spices" mixture used for seasoning meats, soups, and stews as well as homemade sausages and pâtés.

1 tbsp white peppercorns	2 tsp freshly grated nutmeg
1 tbsp black peppercorns	2 tsp ground ginger
8 whole cloves	

Grind peppercorns and cloves together in a spice mill or electric coffee grinder. Combine with nutmeg and ginger, and store in an airtight container.

Storing and Preparing Spices

The fragrance and pungency we value in spices come from their essential oils, which are released when spices are ground, crushed, or heated. For culinary use, most spices are best bought as fresh as possible in their whole form, and ground just before using. The difference between freshly ground cloves, say, and a box of the commercially ground spice is quite astonishing. There are a few very hard spices, like turmeric and dried ginger, that are most conveniently bought already powdered.

With all spices, whole or ground, buying little and frequently is the best policy. All spices should be stored away from heat and light, so avoid placing spice racks near a window or stove. Ground spices should be cleared out every six months or so and replaced with fresh. Well-kept whole spices will have a longer life.

Whole spices can be ground in a spice mill or with a mortar and pestle, preferably ceramic or the metal Japanese sort that has fine ridges on the inner surface. Alternatively, an electric coffee grinder kept especially for the purpose is the easiest of all. Clean the coffee grinder by processing fresh bread after use. A small mesh tea strainer is also handy for sieving freshly ground spices.

Dhal Soup

Tiny red or orange lentils are used in this Indian recipe for a warming and nutritious soup. Spicy flavors are intensified by the typically Eastern technique of stir-frying seasonings before adding them to the soup base.

---

1 1/4 cups red lentils
5 cups light chicken stock
2 tbsp cooking oil
2 tsp black mustard seeds
1 onion, finely chopped
1 clove garlic, crushed
1 tbsp curry powder (see p. 11)

Boil lentils in chicken stock over low heat until very soft. Liquidize or pass lentils through sieve. Heat oil, and fry mustard seeds, onion, and garlic until onion is golden, then add curry powder and cook while stirring for another minute. Add lentils to fried mixture, and heat. If soup is too thick, add more stock or water.

Ginger Glazed Carrots

Ginger, honey, and a touch of pepper add variety to a reliable vegetable that is sometimes considered dull.

1 lb fresh carrots	2 tsp ground ginger
1¼ cups chicken stock	pinch of cayenne pepper
	3 tbsp honey

Scrape carrots, cut into batons, and place in deep skillet with chicken stock, ginger, and cayenne. Cover and simmer until carrots are just tender. Remove carrots to a warm dish. Stir honey into cooking liquid and boil for a minute or two, until reduced to syrup. Pour glaze over carrots and toss to coat well.

Bombay Potatoes

Spicy potatoes serve as accompaniment to a curry meal or as an exotic alternative to potato salad, and are delicious hot or cold. Use new potatoes or firm salad types that won't break up in cooking.

1½ lb potatoes	2 tsp cumin seeds
4 tbsp cooking oil	2 tsp black mustard seeds
1 onion, finely chopped	2 tsp curry powder (see p. 11)
1 clove garlic, finely chopped	

Boil potatoes in skins until just slightly underdone. Cool quickly in cold water, peel, and cut into 1-inch dice. Heat oil and stir-fry onion, garlic, cumin, and mustard seeds until seeds start to pop. Add curry powder and diced potatoes and continue frying for a further 5 minutes, adding a little water to prevent sticking.

Pickled Beets

The deliciously spicy sweetness of homemade pickled beets will convert anyone who has been put off by vinegary commercial ones. Serve hot and freshly made as a vegetable or cold as accompaniment to cold meats, salads, and sandwiches.

---

1 1/2 lb beets, topped and tailed
1/2 cup red wine vinegar
4 tbsp sugar
1 1/2 tbsp pickling spice (see p. 12)

If beets are larger than golf-ball size, slice or cut in quarters. Boil beets until tender and reserve 1 cup resulting beet stock. In a stainless-steel or non-metallic pan, gently heat 1 cup beet stock with vinegar and sugar, stirring until all is dissolved. Tie pickling spice into cheesecloth, put into liquid with prepared beets, and barely simmer for five minutes. Remove from heat and allow to cool. Remove spices, transfer beets and their liquid to a tightly lidded jar, and store in refrigerator.

Sweet and Sour Red Cabbage

Vinegar in this recipe not only balances the sweet spicy flavors but preserves the bright ruby coloring of the cabbage during its slow cooking. This cheering winter dish is the traditional accompaniment for roast pork, game, and Christmas goose.

---

2 tbsp butter or drippings
1 large onion, chopped
2 lb shredded red cabbage
1/2 cup brown sugar
1 tsp ground allspice
pinch of ground cloves
1 tsp salt
1 2/3 cups red wine
3 tbsp red wine vinegar
1 2/3 cups stock or water

Heat fat in flameproof casserole and sauté onion until soft. Add remaining ingredients, pressing down cabbage as much as possible and cover tightly. Simmer 1 1/2 to 2 hours, checking occasionally and adding liquid as needed. Taste and adjust seasoning before serving.

Malaysian Fish Curry

Fish curries are not so well known in the West, but are quick and easy to make. Use firm whitefish that won't break up in cooking: haddock, turbot, brill, and monkfish are all suitable.

---

2 tbsp cooking oil
1 onion, thinly sliced
5 anchovy fillets, chopped
3 tbsp curry powder (see p. 11)
3 tbsp ground almonds
1 1/4 cups fish stock or water
juice and grated rind of 1 lemon
1 small can pineapple chunks
1 1/2 lb whitefish fillets, in chunks
2 tbsp finely chopped coriander leaves or fresh parsley

Heat oil and sauté onion until just golden. Add anchovies, curry powder, and ground almonds and stir fry for 1 to 2 minutes, then add stock or water, lemon juice and rind. Simmer uncovered for 10 minutes, then add pineapple with its juice and the fish fillets. Simmer for 5 minutes, or until fish is cooked through. Garnish with chopped coriander or parsley.

Crab Cakes

Golden brown crab cakes are appealing for family suppers or made in tiny sizes for party fare. Frozen crabmeat works well in this recipe when fresh meat is not available.

1 cup bread crumbs	pinch of ground ginger
1 lb crabmeat	tiny pinch of ground cloves
1 tbsp mayonnaise	salt
1/4 tsp mustard powder	2 tsp baking powder
pinch of cayenne pepper	1 egg, beaten
	fat for frying

Put aside 4 tablespoons bread crumbs, then combine remainder with all the other ingredients except fat. Mix well and form into patties, rolling each in the reserved bread crumbs. Fry in shallow fat until golden brown on each side. Serve with tartar sauce.

Sole Epicurean

Simple fish fillets are given gourmet treatment with a subtly spiced butter-and-lemon sauce. This recipe also adapts well for use with lobster tails and jumbo prawns, as well as more economical fish.

4 fillets of sole	juice of 1 lemon
salt	1 tsp chopped tarragon leaves
paprika	1 tsp coriander seeds, crushed
6 tbsp butter	1/2 tsp ground white pepper

Season sole fillets with salt and paprika. Melt butter with remaining ingredients and heat just to boiling point. Allow to cool slightly. Place sole skin-side down on grill rack, and brush with butter mixture. Grill until golden, then turn fillets and baste again. When fillets are grilled on both sides, serve with remaining butter mixture spooned over.

Fish and Saffron Cassoulet

This French country dish has origins in the saffron- and garlic-growing areas between France's southern rivers and seacoast. The beans can be cooked in advance, leaving fish and breadcrumbs to be added nearer serving time. Any firm whitefish, or a mixture thereof, is suitable.

---

1 tbsp cooking oil	12 oz dried kidney beans,
3 smoked bacon rashers,	soaked overnight
chopped	large pinch of saffron
1 large onion, thinly sliced	salt, pepper
2–3 cloves garlic, crushed	1 lb boneless fish fillets,
2¹/₂ cups fish or	in chunks
chicken stock	generous handful toasted
1¹/₄ cups dry white wine	bread crumbs

Heat oil in large flameproof pot and cook bacon, onion, and garlic briefly; add stock, wine, and soaked beans and bring to a boil. Lower heat, stir in saffron, and simmer, covered, until beans are cooked. Mash beans a little with fork to thicken mixture and season to taste with salt and pepper. Put in fish chunks and cook gently until done, 15 to 20 minutes. Top with bread crumbs.

Saag Gosht

Aromatic seasonings combine with slowly cooked lamb and spinach in a classic Indian dish.

---

2 tbsp cooking oil
1 lb boneless lamb, cubed
1 large onion, finely sliced
1 clove garlic, finely chopped
3 tbsp curry powder (see p. 11)
12 oz spinach leaves, chopped
salt
1 cup plain yogurt

Heat oil in a pan and brown lamb with onion and garlic. Add curry powder and cook for a further 2 minutes, while stirring. Add spinach and salt and continue stirring until spinach is wilted. Stir in yogurt, reduce heat, and cook gently until lamb is very tender, 1 to 1 1/2 hours, adding a little water if needed. Serve with rice or naan, the flat Indian bread.

Cantonese Roast Duck

A fragrant marinade lends oriental savor to duck, which is then given a crispy roasted finish. Duck breasts will cook more quickly than leg portions.

---

1 tbsp cooking oil
3 green onions, chopped
2 cloves garlic, crushed
1-in piece fresh ginger, chopped
3 tbsp soy sauce
2 tbsp dry sherry
1/2 cup chicken stock
1 tbsp sugar
1 whole star anise, broken up
6 black peppercorns, crushed
1 duck, quartered

Heat oil, and stir-fry onions, garlic, and ginger until soft. Add remaining ingredients except duck, and simmer for 2 to 3 minutes. Remove from heat and cool. Pour cooked marinade over duck portions in shallow dish, cover, and leave to marinate for several hours. To roast, drain duck portions and cook in oven preheated to 400°F until meat is well cooked and skin is crispy. Marinade can be boiled until syrupy, then strained and served as sauce.

Tamale Pie

Typical Mexican seasonings and cornmeal give a "south-of-the-border" flair to ordinary ground beef. This is a convenient dish to assemble early in the day for baking later, and is suitable for freezing.

3/4 lb lean ground beef
1/2 green pepper, chopped
1 onion, chopped
1 clove garlic, chopped
2 tsp cumin seeds, crushed
1 tbsp oregano
1 can chopped tomatoes
1 cup canned corn kernels, drained
2/3 cup yellow cornmeal
salt, pepper

Preheat oven to 350°F. Heat cast-iron pan, and brown ground beef. Add green pepper, onion, garlic, cumin, and oregano, and cook until onion is soft. Remove from heat and stir in remaining ingredients, seasoning to taste with salt and pepper. Transfer to greased baking dish and cook in oven for about an hour. The casserole should be solid through and crusted on top.

Spiced Beef

This is a recipe with medieval roots, still popular in Ireland at Christmas. It is delicious hot or cold, served with horseradish cream. The spicy cooking stock is traditionally used to make lentil soup.

3 tbsp dark brown sugar	2 tsp ground ginger
1 tbsp each: ground black pepper, crushed juniper berries, crushed coriander seed, ground allspice	1 tsp ground cloves
	4 lb lean corned beef
	1 1/4 cups Guinness stout

Combine the sugar and spices and rub mixture into the meat. Cover and place in refrigerator for 3 to 4 days, turning meat and rubbing in mixture daily. To cook, barely cover with water in a heavy pan with tightly fitting lid and cook at a gentle simmer (in oven or on top of stove) for about 3 1/2 hours. Add Guinness for final half-hour of cooking. Cool in cooking liquid, and serve thinly sliced.

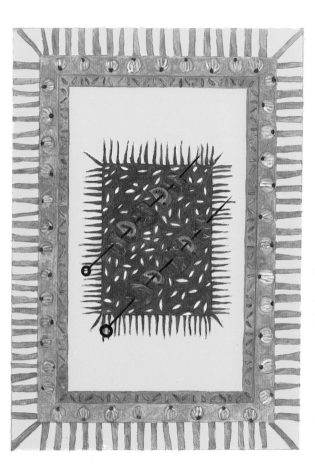

Punjabi Lamb Kebabs

This spicy lamb would traditionally be cooked in a tandoori oven, but is equally delicious cooked on the backyard barbecue or indoors under the grill.

---

1 large onion, chopped
2 tbsp coriander seeds
2 tsp cumin seeds
1 tsp salt
2 tsp ground ginger
2 tsp ground cinnamon
juice of 1 lemon
1 cup plain yogurt
1 1/2 lb trimmed lamb, cut in cubes
8–10 tomatoes, cut in wedges

In a food processor, liquidize onion and spices to a fine paste. Combine with lemon juice and yogurt, pour over lamb, and stir to coat completely. Leave to marinate for several hours. Thread lamb on skewers, alternating with tomato wedges, and cook over high heat on grill, turning frequently and basting with marinade. Serve with rice pilaf.

Chicken Paprika

Sweet red paprika and sour cream are hallmarks of this well-known Hungarian dish, which is excellent served over hot buttered noodles or boiled potatoes to soak up the delicious sauce.

4 tbsp flour	3 tbsp cooking oil
1 1/2 tbsp paprika	8 large mushrooms, sliced
1/2 tsp salt	1 clove garlic, crushed
1/4 tsp ground black pepper	1 cup chicken stock
pinch of grated nutmeg	1 cup sour cream
1 large chicken, jointed	

Combine flour, paprika, salt, pepper, and nutmeg and use to coat chicken pieces. Heat oil and sauté chicken until golden. Add mushrooms and garlic with remaining seasoned flour, and cook for another minute. Pour in stock, cover tightly, and simmer until chicken is cooked, about 45 minutes, adding a little water if necessary. Remove chicken to serving dish and keep warm. Stir sour cream into cooking juices, heat for 3 to 4 minutes without boiling, and pour over chicken in dish.

Ginger Peachy Crumble

This quick-to-assemble dessert is perfect for the summertime peach season, but can be made other times using canned, drained fruit. It is delicious served hot with chilled whipped cream or ice cream.

10–12 peaches, peeled and pitted
½ cup sugar
2 tbsp flour
½ tsp each: ground ginger, ground cinnamon,
ground cardamom
Topping:
1 cup plain flour
6 tbsp butter or margarine
6 tbsp sugar

Preheat oven to 350°F. Slice the peaches, toss in mixture of sugar, flour, and spices, and put into greased baking dish. Combine topping ingredients, rubbing together until resembling bread crumbs, and spoon over peaches. Bake in oven for 30 to 40 minutes.

Elegant Bread-and-Butter Pudding

Real vanilla and a sprinkling of almonds make this bread–and-butter pudding special. Bread that is slightly stale or dry makes lighter-textured pudding.

$^1/_2$ vanilla pod
1 cup milk
1 cup cream
3 eggs
$^1/_2$ cup sugar
10 large slices day-old bread
butter
apricot jam to spread on bread
1 tbsp flaked almonds
confectioners' sugar to dust

Preheat oven to 325°F. Split vanilla pod and scrape seeds into a pan with the milk and cream. Heat just to simmering stage, remove from heat, and allow to cool. Beat eggs and sugar into cooled cream mixture. Trim crusts from bread and spread thinly with butter and jam to make sandwiches. Cut each sandwich diagonally to make four triangles and arrange in slightly overlapping rows in well-greased baking dish. Pour egg and cream mixture over, and set aside for 30 minutes so that bread absorbs liquid. Sprinkle with almonds and bake in oven for 50 to 60 minutes or until knife inserted in center comes out clean. Dust top with confectioners' sugar and serve hot.

Old-Fashioned Pound Cake

This traditional teatime cake with the delicate flavor of freshly ground mace has been updated for quick stirring up in the food processor. As in most cake recipes, the quantity of milk may need adjusting, depending on type of flour used. The batter should have a thick dropping consistency.

1/2 tsp broken mace blades
3/4 cup sugar
1 7/8 cups plain flour
2 tsp baking powder
3/4 cup butter, softened
3 large eggs
5 tbsp milk
1 tsp vanilla extract

Preheat oven to 325°F. Combine mace with 2 tablespoons of the sugar and reduce to powder in a blender. Sift flour and baking powder together and place in food processor with mace mixture and remaining ingredients. Process for three 20-second intervals, scraping down processor bowl between intervals. Baked in greased and lined loaf pan (1 lb) until the cake is golden brown and the centre is cooked through.

Cinnamon Shortbread

Spicy shortbread is even better when baked and allowed to mature for a few days. These universal favorites make excellent gifts and can be made extra special with the addition of chopped almonds or other nuts.

1-in stick of cinnamon	1 cup butter, chilled
1/2 cup superfine sugar	2 scant cups plain flour
3/4 cup rice flour	2 egg yolks
pinch of salt	confectioners' sugar

Preheat oven to 350°F. Grind the cinnamon with a large spoonful of the measured superfine sugar. Combine flours and salt, and rub in butter until mixture is crumblike. Add ground cinnamon, remaining sugar, and egg yolks to make a stiff dough. Press into a shallow, 9-inch square pan, prick all over with a fork, and score into fingers or squares with a knife. Bake in oven for 25 to 35 minutes, until cookies are light brown. Cool before turning out. Store in airtight tin packed with confectioners' sugar between layers.

Date and Spice Crescents

Paper-thin pastry, dates, and cardamom reveal the Middle Eastern origins of these delectable sweetmeats. Filo pastry is sometimes sold in shops as strudel pastry, and is generally found in the frozen-food sections of good supermarkets, delicatessens, and oriental food specialists.

1 cup chopped dates	1/2 tsp ground cardamom seeds
4 tbsp sugar	1/4 cup chopped nuts
grated rind of 1 orange	10 oz filo pastry sheets
3 tbsp orange juice	melted butter
1 tbsp butter	

Preheat oven to 350°F. Combine dates, sugar, orange rind and juice, butter, cardamom, and nuts, and stir over gentle heat until melted together and thickened. Remove from heat and cool completely. Cut filo pastry sheets into 5-inch squares and place in plastic bag to prevent drying out. Brush one square at a time with butter, spread a little filling along edge, and roll up cigar fashion, folding in edges to enclose filling. Gently bend roll to form crescent and place on greased baking tray. Brush with butter and bake in oven until golden brown, 10 to 12 minutes.

Baked Curried Fruit

Tropical fruits and aromatic spices combine in an exotic hot dessert that would be a perfect ending for an Eastern meal.

8 peaches, skinned, pitted and halved	6 tbsp butter
	3/4 cup brown sugar
1 small pineapple, pared and cut in chunks	1 tbsp mild curry powder (see p. 11)
2–3 firm green bananas, sliced	pinch of salt

Preheat oven to 350°F. Lay the prepared fruit in a greased ovenproof dish. Melt butter over low heat and add remaining ingredients, stirring until dissolved. Pour warm mixture over fruit, cover, and bake in oven for 35 to 45 minutes, until fruit is tender. Serve hot with chilled thick yogurt.

Apple Butter

This velvety brown spread is an American favorite, but virtually unknown in Europe. It is an alternative to jam and a good way of using windfall apples.

5 lb firm, tart apples	1 tsp each: ground cinnamon,
6 cups cider	ground allspice,
3 cups sugar	ground cloves

Wash apples, cut out any damaged bits, and chop roughly, with skin and cores. Boil apples in cider until mushy. Press through a sieve

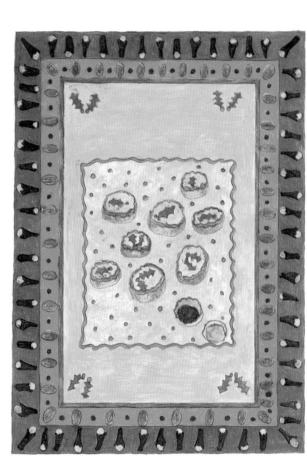

and combine pulp with sugar and spices. Place over very low heat, and cook until purée is very thick and no edge of liquid shows around rim of apple butter in the pan. Pour into hot sterilized jars, seal, and allow to set.

Homemade Mincemeat

Your own freshly ground spices and tangy hand-cut peel lift this Christmas treat to new heights. Two to three months' maturing is sufficient, but a year's wait, with extra topping-off brandy added at the end, is even better.

1 tsp whole cloves
1 1/2 tsp whole allspice berries
1 small nutmeg, grated
2 1/4 cups plus 2 tbsp firmly packed soft brown sugar
3 1/4 cups raisins
3 cups currants
3 1/4 cups sultanas
about 4 cups peeled, cored, and grated sharp apples
2 cups finely chopped suet
1 cup chopped candied citrus peel
1/4 cup candied cherries, halved
scant cup blanched almonds, coarsely chopped
juice and grated peel of 2 lemons
1 cup brandy or Irish whiskey

Place cloves, allspice and nutmeg in a spice mill or electric coffee grinder with 2 tablespoons brown sugar and grind to a fine powder. Wash the dried fruit and combine with the spices and remaining ingredients in a large basin or crock. Mix thoroughly, cover tightly, and leave in a cool place for 24 hours. Mix well again and pack tightly into dry, sterilized jars. Cover mincemeat surface with heavy waxed paper or parchment disks, seal jars, and store in a cool, dark place for at least two months before using.

Apricot Chutney

Rich-tasting apricots combine with apples and spices in this Indian speciality that goes especially well with chicken curries and pilafs. Dried apricots not only give a more intense flavor, but are generally more readily available than fresh apricots.

---

2 cups chopped dried apricots
1 1/4 cups boiling water
4 medium onions, chopped
6 medium apples, peeled, cored, and chopped
1 1/4 cups white vinegar
1 tsp ground mixed spice (see p. 12)
1 tsp ground coriander
1/2 tsp ground ginger
1 tsp salt
1 1/2 cups sugar

Pour boiling water over apricots and leave to soak overnight. Next day, drain and combine with remaining ingredients in a large pan. Stir over low heat until sugar is dissolved. Continue to cook until chutney is thick and jam-like, stirring occasionally and making sure bottom doesn't scorch. Pour into hot, sterilized jars, and seal.

Drinks

Spicy Summer Punch
Spices can also add lift to summery fruit punch.

2½ cups apple juice	½-in piece of dried
1¼ cups pineapple juice	gingerroot
1¼ cups orange juice	½ tsp mixed spice (see p.12)
juice of 1 lemon	2–3 mace blades
2–4 tbsp sugar	2 whole cardamom pods
1-in piece of cinnamon stick	3 cups ginger ale
	or sparkling wine

Combine juices and stir in sugar to taste. Tie spices in a square of cheesecloth, crush with a hammer, and add spice sack to juices. Leave to steep in a cool place for several hours. Remove spices, pour juice over ice in punch bowl, and add ginger ale just before serving.

Aniseed Liqueur
This is one of the easiest liqueurs to make at home, using either the small anise seeds or the very attractive star anise, which can be put in the bottle as a decoration after filtering

2 tbsp aniseed or star anise	¾ cup sugar
2½ cups vodka	½ cup water

Lightly bruise aniseed with a mortar and pestle. Put into a jar with the vodka and leave in a cupboard for 2 to 3 weeks, shaking occasionally. When flavor seems strong enough, strain, and discard seeds. Dissolve sugar in water over low heat, and cool. Combine syrup and infused vodka, pour into clean bottle, and seal.

Index